Weather

REVISED EDITION
Assistant editor Debangana Banerjee
Art editor Shipra Jain
Senior editor Shatarupa Chaudhuri
Senior art editor Nishesh Batnagar
DTP designer Bimlesh Tiwary
Managing editors Laura Gilbert,
Alka Thakur Hazarika
Managing art editors Diane Peyton Jones,
Romi Chakraborty
CTS manager Balwant Singh
Producer Nicole Landau
Producer, pre-production Francesca Wardell
Publisher Sarah Larter
Publishing director Sophie Mitchell
Art director Stuart Jackman
Jacket editor Ishani Nandi
Jacket designer Shreya Sadhan
Consultant John Woodward

ORIGINAL EDITION
Written and edited by Lorrie Mack
Designed by Cheryl Telfer
and Helen Chapman
Publishing manager Sue Leonard
Managing art editor Clare Shedden
Jacket design Chris Drew
Picture researcher Sarah Stewart-Richardson
Production Shivani Pandey
DTP designer Almudena Díaz
DTP assistant Pilar Morales
Consultant Ben Morgan

First published in Great Britain in 2004
This edition first published in Great Britain in 2016 by
Dorling Kindersley Limited
80 Strand, London, WC2R 0RL

Copyright © 2004, © 2016

Dorling Kindersley Limited, London
A Penguin Random House Company

2 4 6 8 10 9 7 5 3 1

001–284733–Feb/2016

ISBN 978-0-2412-2826-5

Printed and bound in China

A WORLD OF IDEAS:
SEE ALL THERE IS TO KNOW

Contents

What's weather?

"Weather" is what the sky and the air outside are like – cloudy, snowy, sunny, or windy. A thick band of air – the atmosphere – surrounds the Earth, but weather only happens nearer the ground, below the cloud tops. This area is called the cloud layer or troposphere.

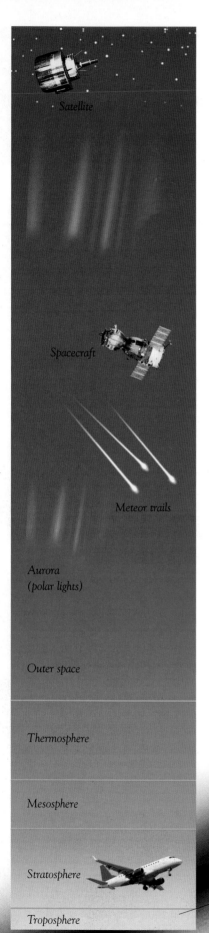

Satellite

Spacecraft

Meteor trails

Aurora (polar lights)

Outer space

Thermosphere

Mesosphere

Stratosphere

Troposphere

Weather facts

● Together, energy from the Sun and moisture in the air create our weather.

● The air has lots of moisture in it because water covers 75 per cent of the Earth's surface.

● Weather kills more people than any other other natural force on the planet.

Thin skin

If the Earth were a huge apple, the whole atmosphere would be thinner than the skin. Driving straight through all its layers in a car, you would reach outer space in about four hours.

The clouds that constantly swirl around the Earth are clearly visible from weather satellites in space.

All our weather goes on in the layer of the atmosphere nearest the Earth – the troposphere.

Out of this world

Above the troposphere is the stratosphere. Here, because the air is very dry, there is no rain or wind. Pilots like to fly at this level because they can be sure of a smooth ride.

When a jet plane flies above the clouds, the passengers have a magical view from the windows.

Every day, we live with one of the most powerful natural forces of all – our weather.

Sunlight

Wind

Frost

Rain

Snow

The seasons

When one part of the world is basking in summer, another part is shivering in winter. This happens because the Earth, which leans to one side, travels on a long journey around the Sun.

On the tilt

The Earth is a round ball that spins around an axis running through the centre (dotted orange line). Because the axis is tilted, the northern and southern halves of Earth take turns leaning in towards the Sun. This creates seasons.

March

It's spring in the northern hemisphere, and autumn at the other end of the world.

SPRING

AUTUMN

Ball of fire

The Sun is a fiery star made of burning gas. We depend on it for light, heat, and energy. Without the Sun, there would be no life on Earth.

SUMMER

Axis

Equator

North and south

The Equator is an imaginary ring around the Earth's middle (yellow line). The area above it is called the northern hemisphere, while the area below it is the southern hemisphere.

WINTER

June

The northern hemisphere is tilted towards the Sun, so the people there are enjoying summer. South of the Equator, there is much less sunshine, so winter is setting in.

A year has 365 days because the Earth

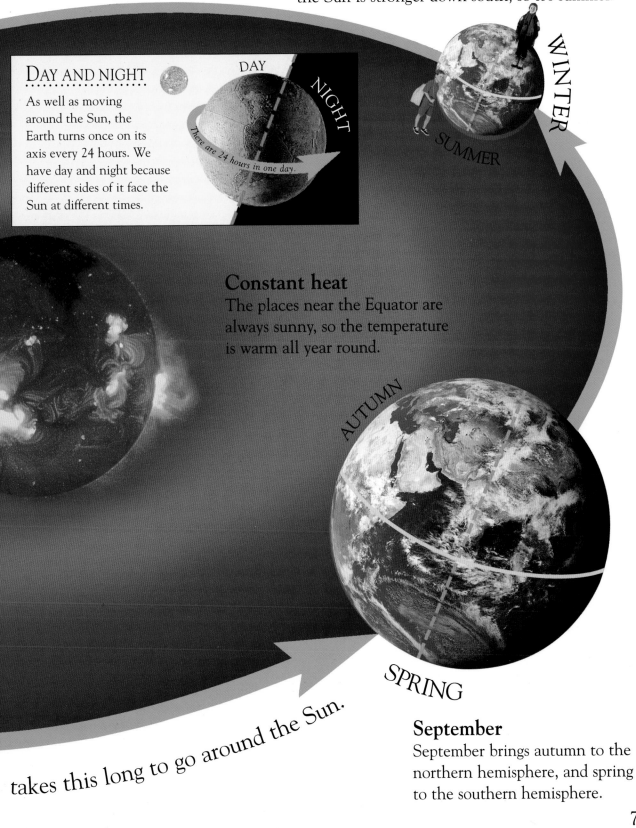

December

In December, the northern hemisphere leans away from the Sun, so it's winter there. But the Sun is stronger down south, so it's summer.

WINTER

SUMMER

DAY AND NIGHT

As well as moving around the Sun, the Earth turns once on its axis every 24 hours. We have day and night because different sides of it face the Sun at different times.

DAY

NIGHT

There are 24 hours in one day.

Constant heat

The places near the Equator are always sunny, so the temperature is warm all year round.

AUTUMN

SPRING

takes this long to go around the Sun.

September

September brings autumn to the northern hemisphere, and spring to the southern hemisphere.

The power of the Sun

The Earth is constantly bombarded with rays from the Sun – a huge ball of burning gases in space. As well as producing heat and light, the Sun controls the Earth's weather.

Warmth and water

Heat from the Sun turns the moisture from leafy trees and plants into invisible water vapour in the air. The same thing happens with the water in lakes and oceans.

Water sometimes turns into water vapour and disappears into the air. This process is called evaporation.

Clouds

Water vapour in the air can turn into tiny droplets that form clouds. The cloud droplets may then join up and become bigger drops of rain.

Wind
The Sun's rays warm pockets of air, which causes them to rise. Cool air then rushes in to fill the gap. This movement of air is what we call wind.

Rain
Water from clouds falls as rain. If the air is cold enough, the moisture turns into snowflakes instead of raindrops. Whatever form it takes, all moisture that falls to the ground is called precipitation.

Starting again
Some rain and melted snow flow back into our rivers and oceans. This water is called runoff. Some will evaporate into clouds once more.

Sunny facts
- If all the Sun's energy could be harnessed for one second, it would power the USA for nine million years.

- The Earth is a tiny dot compared with the Sun, which is big enough to swallow it a million times.

Clouds in the sky

Clouds are made from drops of water. The amount of water in each cloud, its height, and the air temperature, all affect what kind it is. There are three main types – stratus, cumulus, and cirrus – and lots of combinations of these.

Cloudy facts

● In Latin, *stratus* means "layer", *cirrus* means "hair", and *cumulus* means "heap".

● Clouds that have "nimbus" or "nimbo" in their name are rain clouds.

● Clouds that have "alto" in their name form at a medium height.

Cumulus

These clouds are plump and fluffy like balls of cotton wool. Small white cumulus clouds often appear on fine, sunny days, but very big, black cumulonimbus clouds mean rain or snowstorms are on the way.

Stratocumulus clouds have layers as well as the bumpy surface of cumulus clouds. The soft grey shapes often produce drizzle or light rain.

Stratus

Of all the main types, stratus clouds are lowest in the sky. Sometimes they sit right on the ground to form fog. Although stratus means "layer", the layers aren't always clear – often, stratus clouds just make the sky look grey.

Cirrocumulus clouds are a cross between cirrus and cumulus types. When their regular waves of tiny cloud clumps form a pattern that looks like fish scales, we call this a "mackerel sky".

Cirrus

High, wispy, feathery clouds are called cirrus. Here, the air is so cold that clouds are made from ice crystals rather than water drops. Sometimes, strong winds blow them into long strands, or "mare's tails" – so called because they look like horse's tails.

Sky map

Clouds are named according to their height and how they're formed. Even those that look quite similar can have different names at different heights.

Some cumulonimbus clouds are 11 km (7 miles) tall.

Aeroplane contrail

Cirrostratus

Cirrus

Cirrocumulus

Altostratus

Cumulonimbus

Stratocumulus

Cumulus

Nimbostratus

Stratus

Against a blue sky, contrails sometimes look like city streets made of clouds.

Cloud gallery

There is nothing unusual about cloudy skies – most of us see them all the time. But we might be surprised if the clouds looked like flying saucers, sheets of water, or clusters of coloured lights.

Clouds or not?

When jet planes criss-cross the sky, they leave behind long, straight tails of vapour that look like clouds. These are known as contrails.

Wavy nights

Clouds that appear at night and look like waves on the sea are called noctilucent clouds. The name noctilucent comes from the Latin words for "night" and "shine".

Painted clouds

When sunlight passes through the water droplets or ice crystals in a cloud, it can produce beautiful shimmering colours.

Bumpy warning

The peculiar rounded shape of these storm clouds gives them their name. They're called mammatus clouds, from *mamma*, the Latin word for "breast".

Mammatus clouds are often a sign that there's a tornado on the way.

All these bumps are caused by down-currents of air.

Flying clouds

Lenticular clouds got their name because they look a little like lenses, but some of them look more like flying saucers!

Saucer-shaped clouds can hover for hours.

Living in a cloud

Sometimes it's so foggy outside, you feel as if you're walking through a cloud. In a way, you are! Fog is actually a cloud that is sitting on the ground instead of floating in the air. There are several different ways fog is made.

Mist and fog are different types of the same thing – mist is just finer and lighter than fog.

The Golden Gate Bridge in San Francisco, USA, is often surrounded by fog.

Rolling in

When warm, damp air blows over cold land or a cold ocean current, its moisture turns into fog. This is called advection fog.

Mountain mist

On wooded hills, moisture given off by trees turns into fog during the night. By dawn, it has settled into the valleys below. Later, when the Sun warms the air, this moisture evaporates, and the fog clears.

Poison air

When fog combines with smoke, it forms heavy, smelly air. Years ago, Londoners had to live with fogs so thick – even during the day – that people called them "pea soupers". These occurred when smoke from the dirty coal fires that heated most buildings got mixed with fog. Today, a similar condition, known as smog, is caused by pollution from cars and factories.

Hazy days

When the ground loses (radiates) heat and gets very cold, it cools the air above it, making water vapour condense into fine droplets. This creates the most common type of fog, known as radiation fog.

Rain, rain

Clouds are made of tiny droplets of water. When a cloud takes on more and more moisture, the droplets get bigger. Eventually, they get so heavy that they fall to the ground as drops – small ones are called drizzle, and big, heavy ones are called rain.

Scary skies

Rain clouds hold a huge amount of water, which makes them so dense that light can't get through. This is why they look dark and scary. The heaviest rain falls from the biggest, blackest clouds.

How much rain?

Scientists measure rain in a simple gauge set into the ground. After the drops fall through the funnel at the top, they are collected in the main cylinder below.

Average yearly rainfall

Kauai, Hawaii, US
11,680 mm (460 in)

New York, US
1,130 mm (44.5 in)

London, UK
610 mm (24 in)

Berlin, Germany
580 mm (23 in)

Cairo, Egypt
25 mm (1 in)

Arica, Chile
7 mm (0.3 in)

Falling shapes

Most people think raindrops are shaped like teardrops, but they actually look more like squashed buns.

New raindrops are round, but they flatten out gradually as they fall.

Poison rain

When chemicals pour into the air from factories and cars, they react with water vapour to form harmful acids. The result – acid rain – kills forests, poisons water, and even wears away stone.

Deadly showers

When storms hit a river, the raging waters may have enough power to bring strong structures, such as a bridge, down.

White skies

When the air is cold, the moisture in clouds freezes into ice crystals without turning into rain first. These crystals stick together and float to the ground as snowflakes.

There can be as many as 200 ice crystals in one snowflake.

In a really bad blizzard, people can hardly see where they're going.

Swirling curtain

When snow is coming down thick and fast, we call it a blizzard. Sometimes, even when a blizzard is over, wind whip up the snow on the ground so it seems like it's still falling.

White lace

Most snowflakes look like lacy six-pointed stars but some have very different shapes.

These flakes are described as "stellar", meaning star-like.

Snowflakes with six flat sides are called plates.

Columns are long, hollow flakes of snow.

Cosy snow

The Inuit people of the Arctic build small huts from blocks of snow. These temporary shelters, which they use like tents, are called igloos.

Look out below!

Layers of snow can build up so high that a slight movement can topple them over. Tumbling, crashing snow like this is called an avalanche.

A big avalanche can bury people and buildings in seconds.

Snowy facts

● Snow is so important to the Inuit that they have more than 100 words for it, including *piqsiq* (blowing snow) and *auviq* (good snow for igloos).

● In April 1921, 1.93 m (6 ft 4 in) of snow fell in one day at Silver Lake, Colorado, USA.

Fallen snow looks like a white blanket.

Fallen snow looks white and sparkly because it reflects nearly all the light that hits it.

Cold and dry

The heaviest snows fall when the temperature is just below freezing. Very, very cold places hardly ever get any snow.

Icy showers

When solid pellets of ice fall
out of the sky, we call it hail.
Some hailstones are about
the size of plums,
while others are
smaller than peas.

Then it falls, collecting

An ice crystal gets caught in an upcurrent.

*Giant hailstones can
smash through roofs, hurt
people, and flatten crops.*

These hailstones are as big as tennis balls!

Birth of a hailstone

Inside huge storm clouds,
strong, freezing winds whirl
around constantly. Any ice
crystals inside get tossed up and
down, building up more and
more frozen layers on each
crystal. These layers turn the
tiny crystals into hailstones.

Icy missiles

Small hailstones are round and white, but
bigger ones usually have knobbly shapes and
jagged surfaces. The largest hailstone ever
recorded measured 18 cm (7 in) across and
weighed almost 1 kg (2 lb).

The air at the top of a cloud is colder than the air at the bottom.

Each round trip adds another layer of ice.

freezing at the top.

Up it goes again,

moisture on the way.

The ice ball keeps getting bigger and bigger.

until it falls out of the sky.

Falling danger
A single, huge hailstone shattered this windscreen.

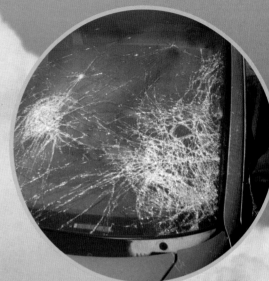

Road risk
Driving through a hailstorm can be deadly. It's hard to see, the road is slippery, and really big hailstones can damage cars and trucks.

Dew and frost

On cool nights, moisture in the air turns into water as it drops to the ground, covering everything with morning dew. On freezing cold days, it hardens as frost.

Dawn sparkle

On cool mornings, you will find glittery drops of dew covering every surface. On this delicate spider's web, the dew drops look like tiny jewels.

Nature's glaze

If the temperature falls after the dew has settled, the moisture often freezes into a covering of clear, smooth ice, like on these berries.

Fern frost

When damp air stays in contact with cold glass, the water vapour turns to ice crystals. These look like fine lace, or the feathery, ferny leaves that give this frost its name.

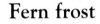

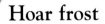

Hoar frost

As water vapour in the air touches frozen surfaces, it sometimes forms spiky ice needles instead of a smooth coating. These spikes are called hoar frost.

Rime frost

During very cold weather, icy winds create a crusty coating, called rime frost, on wet leaves and branches. Because it forms so quickly, rime is thick and hard, with a surface that looks like sugar.

JACK FROST

When feathery shapes appear on windows, and the landscape is white and sparkling, children are told that Jack Frost has been at work with his paintbrush. Jack first appeared in Norse lore as Jokul Frosti (meaning "icicle frost"), son of the wind god Kári. In Europe and North America, he is usually shown as a mischievous elf.

23

Blowing in the wind

Air is restless and moves all the time. When it moves quickly enough for you to feel it on your face, it is called wind. Some winds only blow over a small area – others are part of a big, wavy pattern that covers the Earth.

Magic winds

Bands of high winds, called jet streams, blow around the Earth from west to east. They are so strong that pilots can cut hours off their flight times if they fly along with them.

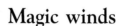

These are wispy clouds caught in the jet stream over northern Africa.

Spinning air

When clouds get caught up in wind, their graceful patterns reflect the swooping, swirling way air sometimes moves.

Wind is just moving air.

Powerful force

It takes strong, steady winds to make a tree grow like this. The winds don't actually bend the trunk, though. They kill all the shoots, buds, and leaves on the side that faces the winds, so only the protected side can grow.

NORTH POLE

Westerly winds

Jet streams

Easterly winds

SOUTH POLE

Near the Equator, winds blow from the east. Further away, they change direction.

Blown away

When desert sand is blown around by fierce winds, it can wear away solid rock. This leaves weird shapes that look like modern sculpture.

Many sand sculptures are top-heavy because wind-blown sand wears away the rock near the ground.

Winds of the world

The Sun's heat and the way the Earth turns create wind patterns. These are so reliable that sailors used them for centuries to cross the oceans.

The lightest winds are called breezes – the strongest are hurricanes.

Windy facts

● When a cold wind is blowing, the temperature feels much lower than it really is. This effect is called the wind-chill factor.

● Wind is measured according to the Beaufort scale, first developed for use at sea. This scale has 13 points: Force 0 is calm and Force 12 is a hurricane.

Electric skies

Lightning bolts are huge electrical charges created when the ice and water inside storm clouds rub together. More than three million of them flash across the skies every day.

Lightning moves at a speed of 37,000 km (23,000 miles) per second.

Lightning facts

● Thunder is the noise lightning makes, but we don't hear it right away because light travels faster than sound.

● One fork of lightning carries enough electricity to light a whole town for a year.

● The names of two of Father Christmas's reindeer, Donner and Blitzen, are the German words for "thunder" and "lightning".

Chosen paths

Lightning can flash either inside a cloud, between a cloud and the air nearby, between two clouds, or between a cloud and the ground below.

When lightning flashes, it makes the air five times as hot as the Sun's surface.

Lightning bolts can be up to 6 km (3.7 miles) long.

Danger!
Never shelter from a storm underneath a tree, since lightning is attracted to anything that stands high above the ground.

Direct hit
Although a lightning bolt lasts only a fraction of a second, its heat is so intense that it can set fire to

Terrible twisters

Tornadoes are terrifying funnels of spinning air. They contain superfast winds with the deadly power to smash houses, flip cars over, and knock trains off their tracks.

Birth of a monster

Tornadoes begin as warm air drawn into the base of huge storm clouds. Warm air is lighter than cool air, so it rises quickly. Then, like water flowing into a drain, it starts to spin. If it spins fast enough, it forms a dark funnel cloud that becomes a deadly twister.

Tornado facts

- At the centre of a big tornado, the wind can reach more than 483 kph (300 mph).

- A tornado can flatten one house, and leave the one next door standing.

- During a 16-hour period in April 1974, 148 twisters hit Dixie Alley, in southeastern USA, killing 330 people and injuring 5,484 more.

Tornado Alley

There are more tornadoes in the central USA than anywhere else on the Earth. In the area where they are most common – known as Tornado Alley – every home has an underground shelter where the family hide when a tornado is on the way.

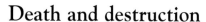 Radar devices like this one can detect signs of a tornado developing inside a storm cloud.

Tracking the twisters

Because they destroy any instruments in their path, tornadoes are hard to study. Special radar dishes, mounted on the back of huge trucks, help to work out where the tornadoes are going.

Death and destruction

Tornadoes destroy property, nature, and human life, all within minutes. Here, a quiet town in the state of Georgia, USA, has been torn apart.

This tangle of crushed metal was once a large, heavy truck.

Deadly storms

Hurricanes are the most violent and
devastating storms on the Earth. They
always build up over warm oceans.
In different parts of the world,
hurricanes are also
known as typhoons
and cyclones.

*Photographed from space,
Hurricane Fran moves
across the Caribbean Sea
towards Florida in 1996.*

*At the centre of every tropical
storm is a small patch of calm,
called the eye. The strongest
and deadliest winds of all spin
around the eye of the storm.*

Monsters from the sea

Hurricanes get their power
from the heat of tropical
seas and because the Earth
turns fastest near the Equator.
They start as small storms,
then build into swirling
clouds of wind and rain.

Lethal water

Hurricanes whip up high, pounding waves. These cause huge damage along nearby coasts and for some distance inland.

Stormy facts

● Hurricanes are graded from 1 to 5. Number 1 is a storm that can cause slight damage, while 5 means a potential disaster.

● Since the 1940s, hurricanes have been given human names. At first they were girls' names only, but since the 1970s, boys' names have been used one year, and girls' names the next.

Run for cover!

When scientists expect a huge storm, they advise people to leave nearby towns and cities. Here, residents of Florida head for safety before Hurricane Andrew hit in 1992.

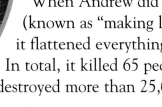

Fatal wind

When Andrew did reach land (known as "making landfall"), it flattened everything in its path. In total, it killed 65 people and destroyed more than 25,000 homes.

Tricks of the light

Every day, the Sun puts on light shows far more dramatic than anything technology has to offer. As well as multicoloured rainbows, it can create magical icebows, shimmering auroras, and glowing spots in the sky.

Ancient legends describe a pot of gold at the end of every rainbow.

Bright colours

Rainbow colours always appear in the same order. Red is at the top, then orange, yellow, green, blue, and indigo, with violet at the bottom. The bigger the rainbow, the brighter and sharper the colours will be.

MAGIC DROPS

Light is made up of seven colours. These are the colours we see in a rainbow. When the Sun shines through raindrops, its light bends and reflects off their surface. The different colours bend at different angles, though. This separates them into the layered bands of light we call a rainbow.

Dazzling displays

Often called "northern lights" or "southern lights" because they appear at the north and south poles, auroras are vast sheets of green streaked with pink and blue. They are caused by electrical storms on the Sun.

Second Sun

Falling ice crystals are able to bend the Sun's rays like raindrops do. This creates large bright spots that look almost like another Sun. Such spots are called sundogs.

Mock moon

If ice crystals fall through the atmosphere at night, they produce a sundog-like effect beside the Moon. These spots are called moondogs.

Frozen light

At the poles, the freezing air often contains tiny falling ice crystals. When sunlight shines through these it can cause an icebow. The crystals do not split the light into different colours, so icebows look white.

All at sea

The ingredients that make up our weather – such as temperature, water, and wind – work in the same way at sea as they do on dry land. But the end results are often very different.

Winds and waves

The winds that blow over our oceans are really strong because there are no large obstacles to slow them down. These powerful winds push the seawater into waves. During big storms, huge waves can reach the top of a lighthouse.

Iced water

Icebergs are huge chunks of ice that have broken off glaciers at the North and South poles. Here, the seas are so cold that icebergs can stay frozen for hundreds of years.

You can only see the tip of an iceberg – most of it is underwater.

Centuries ago, sailors thought waterspouts were blown by huge sea monsters.

Waterspouts

When they form at sea, whirlwinds and tornadoes are called waterspouts. They are rarely as powerful as tornadoes, but big ones can be dangerous to ships.

Fog banks

If warm, moist air blows over cold seas, thick fog forms in high mounds called banks. This fog is very dangerous for sailors, as they can't tell where they're going or what's in front of them.

Desert worlds

Rainy days may make you miserable, but people who live in desert regions would give anything for a bit of rain. Deserts – which can be cold as well as hot – are places where there is almost no rain at all.

Green islands

An island of greenery, called an oasis, sometimes springs up in the middle of a desert. This happens when underground springs seep up to the surface, making it possible for plants to grow.

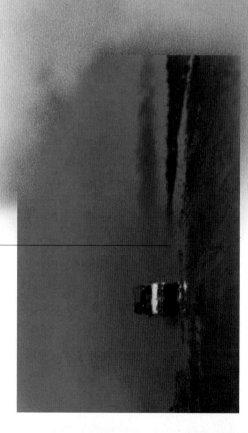

Desert travellers often think they see water in the distance when there is really only sand.

Seeing things

Heat rising up from the ground can make light shimmer so it looks like shallow water. This false image is called a mirage.

Whirling clouds

When desert ground gets hot, the air above it can swirl upwards to form spirals as high as 100 m (328 ft). If dust or sand is sucked into these whirlwinds, they're known as dust devils or sand devils. Australians call them "willy-willies".

Thirsty stems

Desert plants are specially adapted for dry weather. Cacti, for example, are thick and fleshy so they can keep moisture inside them for a very long time.

Dry storms

A lot of desert land is made of sand instead of soil. When the wind blows hard, it creates swirling clouds of choking, blinding sand and dust. At their worst, sandstorms cause more damage than the thickest blizzards.

Weird weather

No matter how much we learn about the weather, it can still come up with a few surprises. Have you ever seen a mud shower, an ice storm, or a black sky in the afternoon?

Blankets of black

As volcanic clouds spread, they block out the Sun. This dark sky hung over the Philippines in 1991, when Mount Pinatubo erupted, covering everything in grey ash.

Exploding Earth

When hot gas and liquid rock burst through the Earth's surface, we call it a volcano. These explosions pour huge amounts of dust and ash into the air.

It's raining mud

When dust storms, or volcanic dust and ash, get mixed up with rain, the result is falling mud. This messy shower is another result of Mount Pinatubo's 1991 eruption.

Mischievous boy

Every few years, a warm ocean current appears off South America. Known as "El Niño" (the Boy Child) because it comes at Christmas, this current upsets weather systems all over the world.

Angry ocean

El Niño warms the seas off California, USA. This causes violent storms along the coast and as far inland as Nevada, 322 km (200 miles) away.

Ice storms

Rain that falls through freezing air forms a layer of clear ice when it lands. This coating, or glaze, can be heavy enough to bring down telephone and electricity poles. When these poles came down in Oklahoma, USA, in 2007, thousands of families lost their power.

Weather forecasting

Nobody wants to have a picnic in the rain, or go to the seaside when it's cloudy and cold. To help us make plans, we depend on weather forecasts. Daily forecasts are quite accurate, but working out what the weather will do over weeks and months is much harder.

Up, up, and away
Watched by curious penguins, this scientist is releasing a weather balloon over Antarctica. The instruments attached to it measure temperature, wind, and moisture, and radio the results back to the Earth.

Ground stations

All over the world – on land, like this one, and in the middle of the sea – weather stations gather information. This is then passed on to scientists in individual countries so they can forecast their weather.

This weather station is in the northwestern state of Idaho, USA.

Forecasting facts

● Weather balloons rise because they're filled with hydrogen or helium gas, both of which are lighter than air.

● Hygrometers measure moisture in the air. The first one was built by Leonardo da Vinci in the 1400s.

Weather satellites

Hundreds of weather satellites orbit the Earth, recording pictures and data. Some move at the same speed the Earth turns, so they stay above one spot. Others fly around the planet from pole to pole.

The first weather satellites were launched in the 1960s.

View from space

Shown as a bright green swirl on this satellite image, a hurricane hits the Gulf Coast of the USA.

Weather wizardry

Huge supercomputers take in weather data from all the available sources. This is fed into a model of our atmosphere so the computer can work out what effect it will have on the weather.

41

Changing climates

The world's weather changes naturally over time. But experts are afraid that pollution is damaging our atmosphere and altering our climates in a bad way.

Poison in the air

These Italian children wear protective clothes to protest against traffic pollution. Toxic gases from cars and factories trap too much heat in the atmosphere. Scientists think this leads to a process called "global warming" – a gradual increase in the average temperature of the Earth's atmosphere. Because these toxic gases act like glass in a greenhouse, they are called "greenhouse gases".

Burning coal creates pollution.

Pollution leads to global warming.

Black power

Along with exhaust fumes from cars, trucks, and buses, a main source of air pollution is smoke. Fossil fuels (such as coal) create the most smoke when they are burned to produce electricity.

Rising water

When the temperature rises by even a little, polar ice-caps start to melt and affect our oceans. Scientists are afraid that if too much ice disappears, polar bears will lose much of their hunting ground.

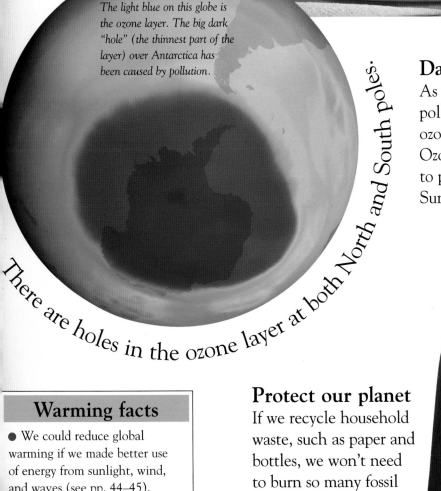

The light blue on this globe is the ozone layer. The big dark "hole" (the thinnest part of the layer) over Antarctica has been caused by pollution.

There are holes in the ozone layer at both North and South poles.

Dangerous exposure

As well as warming the air, pollution damages the layer of ozone that surrounds the Earth. Ozone is a bluish gas that helps to protect the Earth from the Sun's harmful ultraviolet rays.

Protect our planet

If we recycle household waste, such as paper and bottles, we won't need to burn so many fossil fuels to make more.

Warming facts

● We could reduce global warming if we made better use of energy from sunlight, wind, and waves (see pp. 44–45).

● Buying smaller cars – and walking when we can – will also help us to reduce greenhouse gases because we won't create as much exhaust fumes.

Harnessing weather

Whether it feels like a friend or an enemy, weather is something we usually can't control. But today's scientists are learning how to convert its awesome power into cheap, clean energy.

Ancient knowledge

For centuries, wind has carried balloons and kites through the air, and pushed sailing boats across lakes and seas.

Passengers and equipment travel in a small basket suspended from the hot-air balloon.

Powerful facts

- Electricity generated by water (waves, tides, or waterfalls) is known as hydroelectric power.

- The biggest solar power station in the world is in the Mojave Desert, California, USA.

- A large area of land covered with wind turbines is called a wind farm.

Solar power stations need to be built in sunny places.

Catching the Sun

This type of solar power station uses huge mirrors to concentrate the Sun's rays. The heat that the mirrors create is used to generate electricity.

Puffs of wind

These tall turbines are modern windmills that use the wind to produce electricity. Each turbine generates only a small amount of power, but added together they can produce enough to meet the needs of a small town.

Wave power

Remote areas, such as the Scottish island of Islay, often have no mains power. In such places, scientists are working on ways of turning the immense force of breaking waves into electricity. This could be a useful source of energy on ocean shores.

Machinery designed to harness waves has to withstand the roughest seas.

True or false?

How much have you learned about weather? Can you spot which of these statements are true and which are false?

The Sun is a fiery star made of burning rock.
See page 6

A wind turbine can generate enough electricity to power a large city.
See page 45

There can be as many as 200 ice crystals in one snowflake.
See page 18

Sand sculptures are top heavy as wind wears away the rock near the ground.
See page 24

Central USA experiences the most tornadoes on Earth.
See page 29

Rainbow colours can appear in two different orders.
See page 32

Pilots like to fly aeroplanes in the troposphere.
See page 5

Big, black clouds that can bring rain are called cumulonimbus.
See page 10

Toxic gases from cars trap heat inside the atmosphere.
See page 42

It takes the Earth 364 days to go around the Sun.
See pages 6–7

The poison rain that can kill trees in a forest is called sour rain.
See page 17

Which way?

Answer each question correctly to reach Antarctica in order to study the hole in the ozone layer.

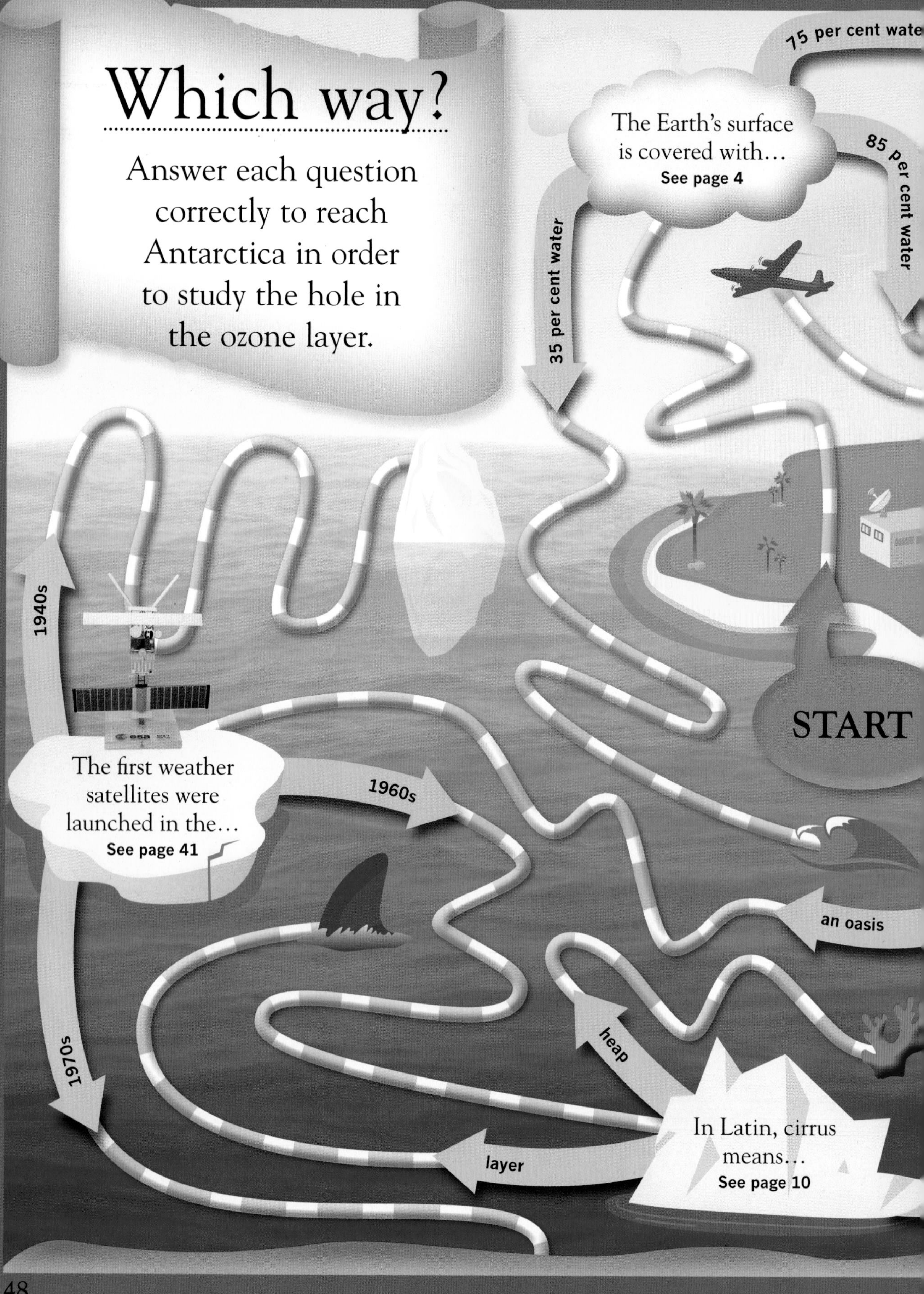

75 per cent water

The Earth's surface is covered with…
See page 4

85 per cent water

35 per cent water

1940s

The first weather satellites were launched in the…
See page 41

1960s

START

an oasis

1970s

heap

In Latin, cirrus means…
See page 10

layer

hailstorm

Mammatus clouds are often a sign of an approaching…
See page 13

cyclone

tornado

stellar

A snowflake with six flat sides is called a…
See page 19

a dune

An island of greenery in the middle of a desert is called…
See page 36

a mirage

plate

column

hair

FINISH

What's this?

Take a look at these close-ups of things from the book and see if you can identify them. The clues should help you!

☀ This forms when water vapour in the air touches frozen surfaces.

☀ It is made up of spiky ice needles.

See page 22

☀ These are bands of high winds that go around the Earth.

☀ Wispy clouds can get caught in them.

See page 24

☀ This is thick and fleshy, and can retain moisture for a long time.

☀ It is specially adapted for dry weather.

See page 37

☀ This is made of blocks of snow.

☀ The Inuit people of the Arctic build this.

See page 19

☀ This is at the centre of every tropical storm.

☀ The deadliest winds spin around this central point.

See page 30

* This is a bridge in San Francisco, USA.
* It is often found covered in fog.

See page 14

* These form inside huge storm clouds.
* They are solid pellets of ice.

See page 20–21

* These are dazzling displays of light.
* They are caused by electrical storms on the Sun.

See page 33

* This is made of huge mirrors to focus the Sun's rays.
* It needs to be built in a sunny place.

See page 44

* This can detect a tornado developing inside a storm cloud.
* It is mounted on a huge truck.

See page 29

* These break off of glaciers at the North and South poles.
* Only their tips can be seen above water.

See page 35

51

Balloon race

Have a hot-air balloon race with your friends across Tornado Alley. See who reaches the finish line first!

Clear skies.
Move forward 4

Refuelled
in a town.
Move forward 2

Deadly tornado
on the way.
Miss a go

Low on fuel.
Miss a go

Winds in
your favour.
Move forward 5

How to play

This game is for up to four players.

You will need
- A dice
- Counters – one for each player.

Move down   **Move up**

Trace over the balloon outlines, or cut and colour your own from card. Each player takes turns to throw the dice, and begins from the START box. Follow the squares with each roll of the dice. If you land on an instruction, make sure you do as it says. Good luck!

FINISH
You are a winner!

Dust storm!
Miss a go

Hailstorm ahead!
Move back 3

Catch a wind current.
Move forward 3

Lightning!
Move back 2

START

Stop to do some sightseeing.
Move back 4

Glossary

Here are the meanings of some words that are useful
to know when you're learning about the weather.

Acid rain Rain that has
been poisoned by pollution

Atmosphere Layers of air that
lie between planet Earth
and outer space

Aurora Bands of coloured light
that appear in the sky over
the North and South poles

Blizzard Storm in which
thick snow falls fast and hard

Cloud Mass of water droplets
or ice crystals in the sky

Condensation Process
that makes water vapour
turn into liquid water

Current Ribbon of moving
water in an ocean

Desert Dry region that
gets very little rain

Dew Drops of moisture that
condense near the ground
after a cool night

Equator Imaginary line
around the middle of the
Earth, between the two poles

Evaporation Process that makes
water turn into vapour, which
vanishes into the air

Fog Cloud that is sitting on the
ground. Thin fog is called mist;

Red sky at night, shepherds' delight

fog mixed with smoke
is called smog

Freezing Process that
makes water turn into solid
ice at 0°C (32°F)

Frost Ice crystals that form
when moisture in the air freezes

Global warming Gradual
increase in temperature of
climates around the world

Hail Pellets of ice that fall to
the ground from storm clouds

Hurricane Powerful storm
that brews up over tropical
oceans. In different parts
of the world, hurricanes are
called typhoons and cyclones

Ice Water that gets so
cold it is frozen solid

Lightning Flash of
electricity in the sky,
caused by a thunderstorm

Precipitation Moisture released
from the air onto the Earth's
surface. Rain, snow, and hail
are all forms of precipitation

Pollution Any substance
that makes air, earth, or
water dirty or poisonous

Rain Drops of condensed
water that fall from a cloud.
Small, fine droplets of rain
are known as drizzle

Rainbow Bands of coloured
light formed when sunlight
shines through raindrops

Snow Clusters of ice
crystals that freeze directly
from vapour, without turning
into drops first. Ice crystals
stick together to form
snowflakes before they fall

Stratosphere Layer of
the Earth's atmosphere
above the Troposphere

Tornado Spiral of air whirling
upwards at very high speed

Troposphere Layer of the
Earth's atmosphere directly
above the ground. All weather
takes place in the Troposphere

Wind Movement of air from
one place to another

red sky in the morning, shepherds' warning.

Index

Acknowledgements

Dorling Kindersley would like to thank:
Janet Allis for her original Jack Frost illustration; Laura Roberts and Pilar Morales for their help with the main Season's artwork; Fleur Star for her general editorial and research assistance, and Penny Arlon for proofreading.

Picture credits

The publisher would like to thank the following for their kind permission to reproduce their photographs:
(Key: a=above; c=centre; b=below; l=left; r=right; t=top)

Alamy Images: Brand X Pictures 6-7; Bryan & Cherry Alexander Photography 19br, Steve Bloom Images 4-5a; Cameron Davidson 31b; EuroStyle Graphics 12bl; Dennis Hallinan 14-15; Image State 3r, 21; Hans-Peter Moehlig 12tl; Plainpicture 43br; A. T. Willett 21br, 26-27b, 19trb; Jim Zuckerman 28. **Ardea London Ltd:** Eric Dragesco 19cl; Steve Hopkin 22bl; D. Hurst 53tr, 58tr, 59c (Ice Cubes). **Bruce Coleman Ltd:** 11tr. **Corbis:** 8t, 10-11; Phil Banko 36tl; Tom Bean 25tr; Gary W. Carter 22c; 1996 Corbis/ Original image courtesy of NASA 24tl, 24cr; Rick Doyle 34-35; Frank Lane Picture Agency 20tl, 41bl; Raymond Gehman 15bl; William Manning 8-9; John M. Roberts 5bra; Galen Rowell 13br; Scott T. Smith 23; Ray Soto 35tr; Stocktrek 41cr; Hans Strand 43tr; Sygma 29cr; Craig Tuttle 22tl; Martin B. Withers; Michael S. Yamashita 18; Warren Faidley 59c, 59c (Palm Trees), 59bl, Klaus Mellenthin / Westend61 50cr, Jim Reed / Sygma 50bl, 51c. **Dorling Kindersley:** ESA 48cl, NASA 50cl, 58br, Mike Webb 47c. **Dreamstime.com:** Akinshin 59fclb, Andrew Buckin / Ka_ru 58bl, Catalina

Zaharescu Tiensuu 50tr, Deyangeorgiev 52cr, Fottoo 52bl, Gorbva 58ca, Juemic 59cb, Kmitu 58clb, Luchschen 58cl, Melissaf84 53br, Stanko Mravljak / Stana 59fcrb, Specular 58cr, Peter Wollinga 59ca, Yekaixp 58cb. **FLPA - Images of nature:** C. Carrolho 33b; Tom & Pam Gardner 36bc. **Fotolia:** Beboy 59cb (Volcano), dundanim 47bl, 58cra, Elenathewise 59clb, Pekka Jaakkola / Luminis 4bl, 47tr, Alexandr Ozerov 58c. **Getty Images:** Nadia Mackenzie 51cl; **NASA:** International Space Station Imagery 4cla; Alejandro Balaguer 38bl; Jose Louis Banus-March 48l, r; Tom Bean 9t; Rob Casey 5br; J.P. Fruchet 24-25, 48c; Jeri Gleiter 44tl; Lester Lefkowitz 45tl; Yannick Le Gal 34l; Jens Lucking 5tr; Nadia Mackenzie 44-45; Graeme Norways 10c; Pascal Perret 16- 17; Colin Raw 42-43; Ulli Seer 46-47; Erik Simonsen 26-27t; Oliver Strewe 17tl; Harald Sund 35tl; John Wilkes 16l. **Masterfile UK:** Allan Davey 27tr. **Nature Picture Library Ltd:** Grant Mcdowell 37bl; Anup Shah 1. **NASA:** 6tr, 6bl, 7tr, 7br. **N.H.P.A.:** Ant Photo Library 36-37. **Oxford Scientific Films:** 39cl; Weatherstock 29tl. Pa Photos: 17r. **The Palm Beach Post/Greg Lovett:** C J Walker 31c. **Jeff Piotrowski/Storm Productions:** 29br. **Photolibrary:** Corbis 52ca. **Planetary Visions:** 41b. **Popperfoto:** 15cr. **Powerstock:** Walter Bibikow 32; Fabio Muzzi 15t; Stock Image 10bl. **PunchStock:** Image Source 53tr (hot-air balloon) **Reuters:** 29bl. **Rex Features:** Sipa Press 38-39, 39tl; Son 27br. **Science Photo Library:** 18tlb; Martin Bond 45cr; Alan L. Detrick 5cr; David Ducros 4-5b; Jack Finch 33tr; Simon Fraser 11tl; R.B.Husar /NASA 39cr; Ted Kinsman 19tcb, 19tl; NASA 30, 43c; Stephen J. Krasemann 33c; Pekka Parviainen 12-13, 22br; Claude Nuridsany & Marie Perennou 2tc, 18tl, 18tlbr, 19tl, 19tc, 19tr; George Post 20-21; Jim Reed 20l, 21tr, 41br; Francois Sauze 13tr; David Vaughan 33cl; Jack Finch 51tr, Ted Kinsman 49cb, NASA 50br, Claude Nuridsany & Marie Perennou 46cl, Jim Reed 51tc. **Still Pictures:** 39br; Denis Bringard 5trb; Angelo Doto 42l; Roland Seitre 40-41.

All other images © Dorling Kindersley

For further information see: www.dkimages.com

Breaking ice

Snow crystal

Cacti

Ice cave

Frost pattern

Altocumulus cloud

Coal fire

Jet stream cloud

Earth

Volcano

Polar bear

Winter landscape

Morning dew

Oasis

Windmill

Cumulonimbus mammatus

Penguin

Trees in early spring

Flooded road

Building destroyed in earthquake

Glacier lake with icebergs

Igloo

Umbrella

Rainbow

Hurricane

Weather station buoy

Frost on berries

Sand dunes

Hot-air balloon

Coal

Clouds during thunderstorm

Factory chimneys releasing smoke

Cumulonimbus

Tornado

Gale

Ice cubes

Crashing wave

Rain gauge

Fog around bridge

Volcanic eruption

Lightning

Stratocumulus

Falling rain

Snowball

Snowfall

Dust devil

Rock structures

Sun

Sunset

Lighthouse